P9-CEM-981

THE UNIVERSAL USE OF CABALA

Traditionally, dating back to at least medieval Europe, the chief *magical* use of the cabala—which is sometimes termed the "practical cabala"—is the making and consecration of talismans. But aside from magic, the primary use seems to be for meditation, the simplest form of which is to use one of the many names of God as a mantra. Even this technique has its own kind of magical application, however: you can achieve a magical effect simply by repeatedly intoning a divine name that is germane to the desired result.

But that is only a small part of it. The cabalistic system is universally applicable in a surprising variety of fields which are usually not associated with anything of the kind. As symbols of universal validity and Truth, the cabala and the Tree of Life are present in the collective unconscious of everyone, even if they never heard of it. If the cabala is present as a system of archetypes in the unconscious of every individual, then it is not hard to see how it can apply to virtually every area of occult and mental endeavor; not only magic (including Witchcraft) but also divination and augury, character reading, and dream interpretation.

About the Author

David Godwin, born in 1939 in Dallas, Texas, and a one-time resident of Houston, Atlanta, Miami, and New York, is a student of esoteric lore, magic, and the cabala. He holds a Bachelor of Journalism degree from the University of Texas at Austin.

The author of *Godwin's Cabalistic Encyclopedia* and compiler of the index to the current edition of Israel Regardie's *The Golden Dawn*, Godwin's articles have appeared in *Gnostica, Llewellyn's Magickal Almanac, Fate,* and elsewhere. Godwin is currently senior editor at Llewellyn Publications.

To Write to the Author

If you wish to contact the author or would like more information about this book, please write to the author in care of Llewellyn Worldwide and we will forward your request. Both the author and publisher appreciate hearing from you and learning of your enjoyment of this book and how it has helped you. Llewellyn Worldwide cannot guarantee that every letter written to the author can be answered, but all will be forwarded. Please write to:

David Godwin
c/o Llewellyn Worldwide
P.O. Box 64383-K325, St. Paul, MN 55164-0383, U.S.A.

Please enclose a self-addressed envelope for reply, or $1.00 to cover costs. If outside the U.S.A., enclose International postal reply coupon.

Free Catalog From Llewellyn

For more than 90 years Llewellyn has brought its readers knowledge in the fields of metaphysics and human potential. Learn about the newest books in spiritual guidance, natural healing, astrology, occult philosophy, and more. Enjoy book reviews, new age articles, a calendar of events, plus current products and services. To get your free copy of *Llewellyn's New Worlds of Mind and Spirit*, send your name and address to:

Llewellyn's New Worlds of Mind and Spirit
P.O. Box 64383-K325 , St Paul, MN 55164-0383, U.S.A.

LLEWELLYN'S VANGUARD SERIES

The Truth About

CABALA

by David Godwin

Author of
Godwin's Cabalistic Encyclopedia

1994
Llewellyn Publications
St. Paul, MN 55164-0383, U.S.A.

The Truth About Cabala. Copyright © 1994 by Llewellyn Publications. All rights reserved. Printed in the United States of America. No part of this book may be reproduced or used in any manner whatsoever without written permission from Llewellyn Publications, except in the case of brief quotations embodied in critical articles and reviews.

For permissions, or for serialization, condensation, or for adaptations, write the Publisher.

FIRST EDITION
First Printing, 1994

International Standard Book Number:
1-56718-325-5

LLEWELLYN PUBLICATIONS
A Division of Llewellyn Worldwide, Ltd.
P.O. Box 64383, St. Paul, MN 55164-0383

Other books by David Godwin

Godwin's Cabalistic Encyclopedia
Light in Extension
How to Choose Your Own Tarot

Llewellyn Publications is the oldest publisher of New Age Sciences in the Western Hemisphere. This book is one of a series of introductory explorations of each of the many fascinating dimensions of New Age Science—each important to a new understanding of Body and Soul, Mind and Spirit, of Nature and humanity's place in the world, and the vast unexplored regions of Microcosm and Macrocosm.

Please write for a full list of publications.

WHAT IS CABALA?

The first question that usually occurs to people about the cabala is, "What is it?"

The simple answer is that it is a system of mysticism with its origins in Judaism, stemming in part from the "chariot" visions of first-century mystics, in part from Gnosticism and Neoplatonism, in part from the theological speculations of medieval Spanish Jews, and in part from later thinkers. For many centuries, cabala was the accepted form of mysticism and theology within Judaism, but for the most part it has now fallen out of favor in religious contexts. Nevertheless, many rabbis and Jewish scholars still take an interest in it. As a philosophy and as a way of looking at God and the universe, it survives in yet wider quarters. Especially in the form developed by Christian enthusiasts in the Italian Renaissance and by 19th-century Christian and pagan occultists, cabalism retains vast importance as the key to mystical thinking outside of the mainstream and to the practice of ceremonial magic.

Once we have arrived at a provisional definition, the next question about cabala is likely to be, "What is the correct way to spell it?"

The correct way to spell it is with Hebrew letters: קַבָּלָה. The way these consonants are expressed in English is a matter of opinion. The simplest way is QBLH—or *qabalah,* if the vowel-points are taken into consideration—although "Q" is merely the conventional way of representing the hard *k* sound of Hebrew and has little in common with the English letter, which must always be followed by the letter *u.* Consequently, Franz Bardon always spelled the word "Quabalah." The sound, represented in Hebrew by the letter פ, *qoph,* could just as well be represented in English by a *k* or *c.* Other ways to spell the word in English include cabala, kabbalah, kaballah, qabala, qabalah, and so on. I have even seen it spelled two different ways in the titles of two books by the same author. Whether or not the word is to be capitalized also seems to be a matter of preference.

In general usage, *kabbalah* refers to the traditional Hebrew form, *cabala* is used to designate the Christian version of the Renaissance, and *qabala* refers to the later development within the Western Hermetic Tradition. These are not hard and fast rules, however. The Hermetic Order of the Golden Dawn, a Victorian occult/magical society, definitely falls within the third category, yet the adepts of that order almost always spelled the word *kabbalah.* I personally tend to prefer either *qabala* or else the usual spelling in English dictionaries, which is *cabala.*

THE *SEPHER YETZIRAH*

There is no agreement about the origins of the cabala. Tradition says that it was communicated by God to Adam, but scholars prefer to look for origins in the mysticism of Judaism as it existed in the first century CE. The first document that is definitely considered to be the forerunner of cabalism and the basis of all the rest of it is the *Sepher Yetzirah* (Book of Formation), by an anonymous author. Hebrew scholar Gershom Scholem thinks the *Sepher Yetzirah* can be dated to the third century CE.

The *Sepher Yetzirah* deals with the creation of the universe by means of the ten *Sephiroth* (emanations, spheres, lights), which are the archetypal numbers 1 through 10 ("ten and not nine, ten and not eleven"), and the 22 letters of the Hebrew alphabet. Collectively, these are known as the "32 paths of wisdom." Insofar as the book describes creation as a process of emanation from the godhead, it was probably influenced by Gnosticism and Neoplatonism. Its emphasis on the archetypal nature of numbers and the stress on the number ten and the absolute nature of numbers seem to hark back to Pythagoras. It is apparently unique, however, in its emphasis upon the sacred and archetypal nature of the letters of the alphabet.

THE HEBREW ALPHABET

The Hebrew alphabet is shown on the next page. Like some other old alphabets, perhaps most notably the Teutonic runes, the letters have names that actually mean something besides just being the names of letters. It is as if we were to dispense with alphabet books that say, for example, "A is for Apple" and instead started calling the letter itself "Apple." Instead of saying that the word "cow" is spelled "see-oh-dubya," we would say that it is spelled "cat-owl-woman," with each of those words being understood as nothing more, in this context, than the name of a letter. Since the letter names are frequently considered to be helpful in determining the essential nature of a letter or word, they are included in the table.

Although some of the letters, such as *aleph*, *heh*, *vau*, *yod*, and *ayin*, are sometimes used to indicate the *presence* of a vowel, strictly speaking the Hebrew alphabet *has* no vowels. It wasn't until the 10th century CE that the Masoretes of Tiberias on the Sea of Galilee finally perfected the use of a system of points and lines written above, below, and within the letters to indicate vowels (for example, בְּרֵאשִׁית, the first word of the Bible ["In the beginning"], is *bereshith*. Without the Masoretic points, it would be written simply as בראשית).

THE HEBREW ALPHABET

Letter	Name	English	Meaning	Number
א	aleph	'	ox	1
ב	beth	b, v	house	2
ג	gimel	g, gh	camel	3
ד	daleth	d, dh	door	4
ה	heh	h	window	5
ו	vav	v or w	nail	6
ז	zayin	z	sword	7
ח	cheth	ch	fence	8
ט	teth	t	serpent	9
י	yod	y	hand	10
כ, ך	kaph	k, kh	palm or fist	20, 500
ל	lamed	l	ox goad	30
מ, ם	mem	m	water	40, 600
נ, ן	nun	n	fish	50, 700
ס	samekh	s	prop	60
ע	ayin	'	eye	70
פ, ף	peh	p, ph	mouth	80, 800
צ, ץ	tzaddi	ts or tz	fishhook	90, 900
ק	qoph	q	back of head	100
ר	resh	r	head	200
ש	shin	s, sh	tooth	300
ת	tau	t, th	tau cross, mark	400

The second form of certain letters represents the way the letter is written at the end of a word. These "finals" are frequently assigned a larger value.

Of course, these vowel indicators did not exist when the Bible was first written down, so we cannot be certain how Hebrew was really pronounced in Biblical times. Also, a great deal of ambiguity exists as to the real meaning of some words in the Bible; since only consonants were written, some words could be any one of two or three entirely different words distinguished only by their pronunciation; that is, by their vowels. If we had no vowels in English, for example, we could know only from the context whether CT was "cat," "cot," or "cut."

In the English-language occultist and magical literature of the 19th and 20th centuries, the Masoretic points are almost never used when Hebrew words are cited. This may be because they serve only as a confusing complication to someone who doesn't know very much about the Hebrew language, or it may simply be that, until very recently, it was an expensive and time-consuming process—if it wasn't altogether impossible without special fonts and equipment—for typographers to reproduce these diacritical marks. For someone not engaged in producing many Hebrew texts, it would not have been worth the investment.

If you intend to study the Hebrew alphabet, notice that some of the characters are quite similar to each other and are easily confused.

Observe the differences between *beth* and *kaph* (ב and כ); *gimel* and *nun* (ג and נ); *daleth* and *resh* (ד and ר); *heh, cheth,* and *tau* (ה, ח, and ת), *vav* and *zayin* (ו and ז), *teth* and *mem* (ט and מ), *mem* final and *samekh* (ם and ס), and *ayin* and *tzaddi* (ע and צ). If the printing of a text is small or blurred, these similarities can sometimes be very confusing.

The shapes of all the Hebrew letters are said to be derived from the primal *yod* (׳). The shapes of the letters are thought to be sacred and to possess esoteric meaning in and of themselves. This is why the Masoretes invented the system of points and lines that does not actually modify the letters themselves, and why they did not simply invent new letters (for the vowels) that would necessarily have to be of a non-sacred nature.

According to the *Sepher Yetzirah,* the Hebrew alphabet contains three "mother letters," *aleph, mem,* and *shin* (א, מ, and ש); seven "double letters," *beth, gimel, daleth, kaph, peh, resh,* and *tau* (ב, ג, ד, כ, פ, ר, and ת); and 12 "single letters," *(heh, vav, zayin, cheth, teth, yod, lamed, nun, samekh, ayin, tzaddi,* and *qoph* (ה, ו, ז, ח, ט, י, ל, נ, ס, ע, צ, and ק). The three mothers correspond to the three primordial elements, Air *(aleph),* Water *(mem),* and Fire *(shin).* The double letters are so called because they each have two possible pronunciations, designated by the presence or absence of a dot in the middle of the letter. The dot is called a *daghesh*. For example, *peh* can be either *p* (פ) or *ph* (*f*) (פ). The one exception to this is *resh*. If it ever had a pronunciation other than *r*, it has been lost in time.

The *Sepher Yetzirah* says that the seven double letters go with the seven planets (Moon, Mercury, Venus, Sun, Mars, Jupiter, and Saturn) and that the 12 single letters correspond with the 12 signs of the Zodiac. In fact, the planets and the signs—i.e., the cosmos—were *created* by means of these letters. However, the oldest versions of the *Sepher Yetzirah* do not say which letter goes with which planet or which sign; just that the doubles correspond to the planets and the singles to the zodiacal signs. Material added at a later date does sort all this out, but these addenda exist in several different versions that disagree with one another—and all of them are different from the system eventually used by the Golden Dawn.

It is probably not a coincidence that God (i.e., Elohim) is mentioned precisely 32 times in the first chapter of Genesis. There are ten instances of "God said," which correspond to the Sephiroth. Of the remaining 22, "God made" three times (corresponding to the three mother letters), "God saw" seven times (corresponding to the double letters), and God did something else 12 times (corresponding to the single letters).

THE *ZOHAR*

After the *Sepher Yetzirah*, nothing much more is heard about cabala until the twelfth and thirteenth centuries, when various documents of a mystical character slowly began to appear. Among these was a collection of writings known as the *Bahir*. In 1305, the *Zohar* (Book of Splendor) was published in Spain. Bits and pieces of this book had been circulated from time to time by Moses de Leon of Guadalajara. According to him, the *Zohar* had been written in the first century CE by Simeon ben Yochai, a famous rabbi who was said to have hidden from the Romans for 13 years in a cave. It was during this time that he supposedly wrote the *Zohar*.

Many people still believe that Simeon ben Yochai really did write the *Zohar*, although the widow of Moses de Leon said that Moses had written it all himself. Textual evidence seems to indicate a thirteenth-century origin, and, if we assume that Simeon wrote it, we have to explain how he kept coming up in the first century with ideas, concepts, and modes of expression that were contemporary to the thirteenth-century mystical Jewish community in

Spain. No older written version exists than that put forth by Moses de Leon.

For the most part, the *Zohar* consists of dialogues or reports of conversations between famous rabbis, or between them and their students. Part of it—not the most important part, but rather things in the nature of supplementary material—was translated into Latin by Knorr von Rosenroth (a Christian) in the seventeenth century. This translation, the *Kabbala Denudata*, was further translated into English in 1888 by MacGregor Mathers as *The Kabbalah Unveiled*.

THE TREE OF LIFE

It was during the fourteenth century that the diagram known as the Tree of Life or Tree of the Sephiroth became popularized (see illustration on opposite page). According to Idries Shah, the Tree was based on an earlier diagram produced by the Brethren of Sincerity in Basra, Iraq. The Iraqi Tree had only eight numbers (or "Sephiroth"), but two more were added by the Spanish Jewish cabalists to make it conform to the *Sepher Yetzirah*. Whether this is really the case or whether the Tree was evolved independently by the Jewish cabalists is a matter of scholarly opinion.

Be that as it may, the Hebrew Cabalistic Tree of Life has had ten Sephiroth for at least 700

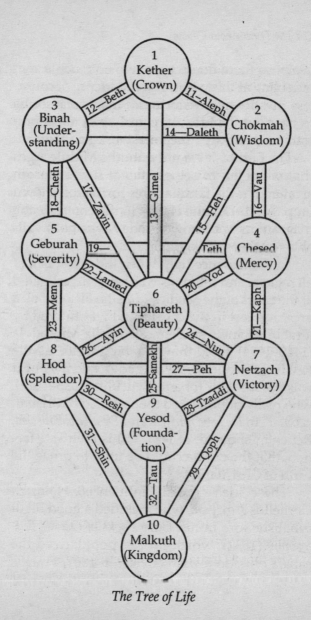

The Tree of Life

years, so there doesn't seem to be much use in quibbling at this point. The experience of countless mystics, meditators, and magicians seems to bear out the idea that the Tree of ten Sephiroth is a perfectly functional working model.

The point is, it is not until the Middle Ages that we begin to see glyphs of the Sephiroth arranged in the familiar Tree formation shown on page 11. Despite claims to the contrary, the diagram as we know it today was not available to Moses or Solomon.

In Renaissance Italy, when the mysticism of all regions and religions was being investigated at the court of the Medici, Marsilio Ficino took a great interest in the cabala, and was tutored by a rabbi. Ficino's student, Pico della Mirandola (1463–1494) took things a bit further at the newly re-established Platonic Academy, but it was *his* student, Johann Reuchlin (1455–1522), who really popularized the so-called "Christian cabala." In *De orbe mirifico* and *De arte cabalistica*, Reuchlin showed, at least to his own satisfaction, that the cabala could be used to prove the truth of Christianity.

These ideas greatly influenced Heinrich Cornelius Agrippa, who included a good bit of cabalistic lore in his *Three Books of Occult Philosophy* (1531), which further popularized the cabala outside Jewish circles. In 1801, Francis

Barrett published *The Magus,* a compendium of occult information, and copied large portions of it from an English translation of Agrippa. Thus the cabala came to be a central pillar of the occult revival of the 19th century, which received its greatest impetus from Eliphas Levi (Alphonse Louis Constant, 1810–1875) of Paris. Levi in turn influenced the founders of the Hermetic Order of the Golden Dawn and, through that, one of the order's members, Aleister Crowley.

In the Western Hermetic Tradition—that is, in the system that begins with the writings attributed to Hermes Trismegistus in the early centuries of this era and which extends through Pico, Reuchlin, Agrippa, Levi, and the Golden Dawn—the cabala is focused upon the Tree of Life as a reference point for everything else. The Tree does not have this central importance in traditional Jewish cabala divorced of its Christian and Hermetic accretions, but it still plays an important part.

The Tree diagram is important for several reasons. First, it is a diagram of how the universe was created by God. A Lightning Flash is said to extend from the first Sephirah (plural = Sephiroth) to the tenth—the Lightning Flash of creative energy proceeding from the eternal unity of God. It also shows the way back to

God, by ascending the Tree. This is said to be the Path of the Serpent, the serpent being a symbol of knowledge and rebirth.

Aside from that, the Tree is also a map of the universe at all levels. The table on the following page lists each Sephirah along with the divine names, archangels, angelic choirs, and planets associated with each.

I suppose it is rather arbitrary to call this diagram a "tree." It bears little physical resemblance to the average oak tree. Nevertheless, it is a tree inasmuch as it has Sephirothic "fruit" branching from a central "trunk." It is not just any tree, of course, but the World Tree, the Yggdrasil of Norse mythology, the Tree of Life (*Etz Chaim*) of the Garden of Eden.

Tree or not, it is also useful to think of the diagram as showing three columns or pillars— the Pillar of Mercy on the right (Chokmah, Chesed, and Netzach), also sometimes called the Pillar of Wisdom because of Chokmah; the Pillar of Severity or Strength on the left; and the Pillar of Mildness or Beauty (because of Tiphareth) in the middle. The middle pillar is also known as the "Middle Pillar," in which case the name implies far more than simply its position on the Tree. The name written with initial capital letters refers to the middle way of mysticism, ascending to deity by way of the

CORRESPONDENCES OF THE TREE OF LIFE

Sephirah	Divine Name (Atziluth)	Archangel (Briah)	Angelic Choir (Yetzirah)	Physical Cosmos (Assiah)
1. Kether (Crown)	Eheieh (or Ehyeh)	Metatron	Chayoth ha-Qadesh	Primum Mobile
2. Chokmah (Wisdom)	Yah	Raziel	Ophanim	Sphere of the Zodiac
3. Binah (Understanding)	YHVH Elohim	Tzaphqiel	Aralim	Sphere of Saturn
4. Chesed (Mercy)	El	Tzadqiel	Chashmalim	Sphere of Jupiter
5. Geburah (Severity)	Elohim Gibor	Kamael	Seraphim	Sphere of Mars
6. Tiphareth (Beauty)	YHVH Eloah va-Daath	Raphael	Melekim	Sphere of the Sun
7. Netzach (Victory)	YHVH Tzabaoth	Haniel	Elohim	Sphere of Venus
8. Hod (Splendor)	Elohim Tzabaoth	Michael	Beni Elohim	Sphere of Mercury
9. Yesod (Foundation)	Shaddai El Chai	Gabriel	Kerubim	Sphere of the Moon
10. Malkuth (Kingdom)	Adonai ha-Eretz	Sandalphon	Eshim	Sphere of the Elements

central column of the Tree rather than taking the right-hand path of the saint or the left-hand path of the dark magician. Both of these side paths are likely to lead the normal person into destruction. The term "Middle Pillar" also refers to a spiritual exercise used within the Golden Dawn.

Above and beyond Kether, the highest Sephirah, is *Ain Soph*, the Infinite, which has no number. It is the unmanifest and inexpressible, God in the most essential aspect. *Ain Soph* is in many ways similar to the Chinese Tao and the *Hen* (One) of Plotinus—anything you can say about it is untrue because any sort of definition whatever necessarily tries to place limits on the illimitable.

In some cabalistic thought, including that embraced by the Golden Dawn, *Ain Soph* is elaborated into the "three veils of negative existence"—*Ain* (nothing), which is the highest and most inexpressible (and least comprehensible to the mortal mind); *Ain Soph;* and *Ain Soph 'Or* (or *Ain Soph Aur)*, the Limitless Light.

THE SEPHIROTH

The English names of the Sephiroth are in several cases not much more informative than the Hebrew names. "Crown" is plain enough; it crowns the Tree. It is the undifferentiated One,

God before creation has taken place. One explanation of the beginning of the process is that God becomes (or eternally is) aware of himself/herself/itself—bearing in mind that God ultimately transcends sexual distinctions altogether—and thus produces Wisdom (Chokmah), the second Sephirah. The point becomes the line.

Crown and Wisdom produce Understanding, Binah, and the "Supernal Triad" is formed. Chokmah is the male principle, the invading seed of potential, the Chinese yang, the so-called Supernal Father. Whereas the God-name associated with the Crown is Eheieh (I AM), Chokmah is called Yah, the first half of YHVH. (Even so, the name embodies glyphs of both male and female principles.)

Understanding is of course just the opposite, the balance for Wisdom. Sephiroth on opposite sides of the Tree represent extremes, but they are always balanced and resolved by a third term. Thus Binah is the female principle, the nourishing and nutritive aspect of creativity, the womb where everything develops after receiving the creative seed of Chokmah, yin, the Supernal Mother. This arrangement, or this understanding, may be a clue as to why priests of the Order of Melchizedek pray to "Father-Mother God."

An Abyss separates the Supernal Triad from the rest of the Tree, but, with the number 4, Mercy, we finally arrive at order and solidity. The line became a surface at 3, but now the surface becomes a solid. The Universe begins to move into manifestation—at least we have three dimensions now, even though nothing solid has yet been created. That is way down the line.

Mercy is balanced by Severity. Mercy lets the serial killer/rapist go free on parole and is opposed to prisons to begin with; Severity wants to execute all felons. The lesson of balance is taught once again. If nothing else, the Tree teaches us the vital necessity of balancing radical extremes.

The thesis and antithesis of these two opposites produces a synthesis in Tiphareth, Beauty. The idea implied—among an infinity of others—is that the balance of mercy and severity produces beauty, a beautiful rulership (as of God, as the ultimate paradigm) or a beautiful parent-child relationship.

But manifestation is not complete, so Chesed and Geburah are reflected, as it were, on a lower level by Netzach and Hod, Victory and Splendor. We can say that, in the Microcosm, these two Sephiroth represent right and left brain activities, respectively—Netzach is creative, intuitive, holistic, whereas Hod is analytical and linear. Hod is the scientist pouring over his statistics in his dark tower, or the computer hacker working out a problem at 3 AM, whereas Netzach is the wild jungle dweller who is still indistinguishable from nature itself—and that includes fang and claw, just as Hod includes the cold, analytical mind that experiments on animals or works out formulae for ever-more-powerful bombs. But that is the dark side of these Sephiroth. On a different level, Netzach is creative inspiration and Hod is workmanlike skill, and this gives a hint as to their meaning on a higher level, within the divine creative process. Herein, a progressive move toward material expression can be discerned.

The actual names of these two Sephiroth may seem puzzling, particularly if you attempt to correlate them with the planetary spheres and then with the Roman gods after whom the planets were named. What does Venus have to do with Victory, or Mercury with Splendor? Anyone who has ever seen the planet Mercury low in the sky on an icy morning might have an idea of the latter, but perhaps it might be more helpful to think of the victory of a creative breakthrough, the triumph of a flash of inspiration, and the splendor of actually fashioning and shaping the product of this prior creative thought.

At any rate, Netzach and Hod are further balanced or synthesized in Yesod, Foundation; or it might be more accurate in this case to say that creation and skill combine to form the foundation of the created world. Although it might appear from its position that Yesod is the foundation of the whole Tree, it is really the foundation of Malkuth, the material world, the end product of divine creation.

And that's what Malkuth, the tenth Sephirah, is: the created universe, the world of the elements. Hanging from the rest of the Tree like a dependent fruit, it is the end result of the emanation of deity. The path from Kether to Malkuth, the instantaneous process of creation, is called the Lightning Flash, or sometimes the Flaming Sword. To return to God, it is necessary to reascend the Tree by the Path of the Serpent, which is not quite the same.

In order to ascend the Tree to the Supernal Sephiroth—which very few people have done except for great mystics, religious leaders, and avatars (incarnations of deity), it is necessary to cross the Abyss. This is the Dark Night of the Soul spoken of by St. John of the Cross. According to the system of the Elizabethan magus John Dee, as elaborated by Aleister Crowley in the early part of this century, the Abyss is inhabited by Choronzon, the demon of chaos, the guardian of the threshold. All who pass that way must confront him without going insane or being turned back. Needless to say, this is far more than the tame imaginative exercise that some have tried to make of it.

According to Kenneth Grant and many others who have taken their direction from him, the horror-fiction writer H. P. Lovecraft (1890-1937) tried and failed to cross the Abyss, and this is reflected in his stories. It is, in fact, just this that lends his tales their fascination and gripping, haunting power despite an adjective-laden prose style that some find antiquated and inept. According to this idea, Lovecraft, despite the philosophy of "mechanistic materialism" that he held to so steadfastly in all his letters and conversations and despite his expressed disdain for magic in general and Aleister Crowley in particular, was secretly a master magician privy to arcane secrets gleaned from an ancient grimoire, the *Necronomicon*. Actually, this tome existed only in Lovecraft's imagination, as a fictional device in his stories, although there have been several volumes published in the last 20 years that purport to be the real *Necronomicon*. In some cases, the perpetrators of these hoaxes have confessed in print, albeit in small-press publications.

According to some cabalists, there is a sort of pseudo-Sephirah or quasi-Sephirah in the Abyss, somewhere between and slightly below

Chokmah and Binah. Without a number, it is called *Daath*, Knowledge. When it is shown on diagrams of the Tree, it is usually outlined with a dotted line. Perhaps this is just a way of saying that knowledge is needed to cross the Abyss.

THE FOUR WORLDS

At the divine level, the Tree shows God in various aspects—God the Father, God the Mother, God the benevolent ruler, God the stern judge, and so on, right down to God as the sovereign of this world. This level of understanding, or this plane, is called the World of Nobility; in Hebrew, *Olam Atziluth*. From the standpoint of creation or manifestation, Atziluth is the World of Plato's archetypes, Ideas in the mind of God. If applied on a lower level, it signifies that stage of the creative process wherein the idea of the project is formulated. The Tree adheres to the Hermetic axiom: "As above, so below." Whatever is true on the divine or cosmic level (macrocosm) is also true on the level of the individual human being (microcosm).

The second level is the World of Creation, *Olam ha-Briah*, where Ideas begin to take shape. In human terms, this is the stage of creation where definite plans are formulated, blueprints are drawn, lists are made. In Briah, each Sephirah is associated with an archangel.

Next comes the World of Formation, *Olam ha-Yetzirah.* From the standpoint of human creation, Yetzirah represents the stage where materials are gathered and all is made ready for the actual process of building, making, or implementing the project. Yetzirah also represents the World of the angelic choirs, such as the seraphim and cherubim.

Finally, we reach the World of Action, the material world, *Olam ha-Assiah.* In terms of divine creation, this is the manifested universe that we see around us. In human terms, it is the actual completion of the project that you got the idea for way back in Atziluth. In Assiah, each Sephirah is associated with some aspect of the material universe that we see in the heavens, from the starry firmament and beyond to the Earth and its four elements of Earth, Air, Fire, and Water, which are all included in the lowest Sephirah, *Malkuth* (Kingdom).

As for how the four worlds relate to the Tree, some authorities assign Atziluth to Kether, Briah to Chokmah and Binah, Yetzirah to Chesed through Yesod inclusive, and Assiah to Malkuth. Perhaps it is more useful and closer to the truth, however, to say that the entire Tree exists completely in all four worlds. Some people say that this constitutes four Trees, the Malkuth of one adjoining the Kether of the next, but it might be more accurate to say that the same Tree exists on four different levels. Of course, I use the word "exist" advisedly. Strictly speaking, the Tree is a map, a symbol, with no objective existence of its own. When you do "pathworking" and travel the paths from Sephirah to Sephirah, you are traveling a part of the astral world with certain characteristics; you are not walking down a ribbon from one circle to another.

ADAM QADMON

Inasmuch as God is said to have created humanity (*adam*) in His own image ("male and female created he them"), it is only natural to assume that the anatomy of the body of God and, indeed, the spiritual reality of the entire universe, should have a human shape, even if only in a symbolic fashion. Again, "as above, so below." In a system that may have come before the arrangement of the Sephiroth into the Tree of Life diagram, cabalists conceived the idea of the archetypal man, or primordial man, Adam Qadmon.

God, as Kether, the first Sephirah, is called *Arik Anpin*, literally "long of nose," an idiom meaning "long on patience." His creation, centered in Tiphareth, is *Zauir Anpin* ("short of nose" = hot tempered). Arik Anpin is also called Macroprosopus, the Greater Countenance, and Zauir Anpin is called Microprosopus, the Lesser Countenance. Malkuth is the Bride of Microprosopus. All this is very similar to the system of emanations worked out by the Neoplatonic philosopher, Plotinus, in the third century CE: The One (God), *Nous* (the Thought of God), and *Psyche* (the World Soul).

THE MICROCOSM

In the World of Assiah, the Tree is manifest not only in the Macrocosm—that is, in the heavenly spheres—but also in the Microcosm, in the individual human being. Furthermore, it is reflected on at least three levels: soul, mind, and body.

The soul has three parts: *neshamah, ruach,* and *nephesh.* This is essentially the Jewish version of Plato's scheme of *logos, thymos,* and *epithymia,* and in some ways these parts are analogous to spirit, soul, and body, but it might be more meaningful to the materialistic modern mind to say that they correspond to the human forebrain, the mammalian mid-brain, and the reptilian hind-brain. In any case, *nephesh* is not the same thing as the physical body, which is called *guph,* but rather represents the animal instincts. *Ruach* is the reasoning faculty, and *neshamah* is the higher soul. On the Tree of Life, *neshamah* corresponds to the Supernal Sephiroth, *ruach* to Tiphareth and the four Sephiroth surrounding it, *nephesh* to Yesod, and *guph* to Malkuth.

Neshamah, the only part of the soul thought to survive death for very long, is further subdivided into *yechidah* (Kether), *chiah* (Chokmah), and *neshamah* proper (Binah). *Yechidah* is the highest part of the soul, the part that partakes of divine nature, the Hindu *atman*, but, strictly speaking, anything above Binah is thought to be incomprehensible to mortals.

The correspondence between the Sephiroth and parts of the human mind is a somewhat more recent invention influenced by modern psychological theories. In this system, the *ruach* is divided into memory (Chesed), will (Geburah), imagination (Tiphareth), desire (Netzach), and reason (Hod).

The physical correspondences of the Tree are, however, well established and of long standing. Kether is the higher soul, somewhere above the crown of the head. Chokmah is the right side of the head, Binah the left side. Chesed is the right arm and Geburah is the left arm, Tiphareth the heart, Netzach the right hip and Hod the left hip. Yesod corresponds to the genitals and Malkuth to the feet. It is helpful to visualize the Tree superimposed on your body.

It may be seen from the foregoing that the Pillar of Mercy is on the right side of the body, considered to be "masculine," yang, the white pillar of the temple, while the Pillar of Severity is on the left, "feminine" side, yin, the black pillar. It may seem odd to find the Sephirah of Mercy on the masculine side and the Sephirah of Severity and war on the feminine side. One normally considers mercy and compassion to be a feminine trait, while it is natural to think of the sword-wielding right arm as Geburah. Similarly, one thinks of the intuitive faculty of Netzach as being feminine and the rational faculty of Hod as being masculine, yet Netzach is on the right (male) side and Hod on the left (female) side.

It must be remembered, however, that "masculine" and "feminine" do not mean the same thing in mysticism as they mean on the material plane. The terms have nothing to do with the human sexes, or with human sexism. It might be more helpful to forget the male-female terminology and just think of yin (dark) and yang (light).

Failure to think in higher terms in this instance apparently caused the leaders of the Golden Dawn—and subsequently Crowley, Dion Fortune, Paul Foster Case, Israel Regardie, and everyone else associated with the Order—to reverse the pillars, so that they placed the Pillar of Mercy on the left side of the body and the Pillar of Severity on the right. Since the Pillar of Severity is plainly the dark left-hand path, yin, and "feminine," it seems as if it should have been obvious that it corresponds to the left side of the body; likewise with the Pillar of Mercy and the right side of the body. The attributions given above are not only intuitively correct, but they are also confirmed throughout the *Zohar*.

The most serious consequence of mixing the pillars this way is that generations of occultists and magicians have been performing the exercise known as the "cabalistic cross" backwards for more than a hundred years. Geburah is plainly the *left* shoulder, not the right, and Gedulah (another name for Chesed) is obviously at the *right* shoulder, not the left.

TETRAGRAMMATON

The four worlds correspond to the four elements (Fire, Water, Air, and Earth), but more importantly to the four consonants of the divine name, Tetragrammaton (the name of four letters), *yod heh vav heh*, יהוה. No one today knows how this name should be pronounced. It has always been forbidden for anyone to even attempt to pronounce the name except for the high priest at Jerusalem, and he only once a year. He was the only one who knew the secret of its proper pronunciation.

The name occurs frequently in scripture, but, when a Jew is reading aloud, he or she must always substitute the name "Adonai" rather than attempt to pronounce יהוה. To remind readers to do this, the Masoretic vowel points for "Adonai" were added to יהוה whenever it occurred, like this: יְהֹוָה. This practice led Christian Elizabethan translators to write the name as "Jehovah," but this is a mistake. Many modern scholars think the name was probably pronounced "Yahweh" or "Yahveh," but that seems too simple and straightforward for a great secret. The written name may be an abbreviation or a code for the real name. No one knows. In magical practice, the name is usually pronounced letter for letter: "Yod Heh Vav Heh."

The consonants of the name also make up a divine family: *Yod* is the Supernal Father, corresponding to the Sephirah Chokmah. (Note that Kether, the Crown, transcends distinctions of gender as well as all other dichotomies.) The first *heh* is Binah, the Supernal Mother. Together they produce *vav*, the Son, who corresponds to Tiphareth (and the five surrounding Sephiroth), and the final *heh*, the Daughter, in Malkuth. In a doctrine similar to some Gnostic ideas, the Daughter, who corresponds to the material world and the Hindu Maya, has to be redeemed by the Son, a saviour figure representing enlightenment.

Reuchlin had no difficulty adapting this story as a Christian allegory and a "proof" of Christianity: the Son, obviously, is Jesus, and the Daughter is the Church. This is not really a great innovation, however, because, at least in some branches of cabalism, Jews already identified Tiphareth with the Messiah, who was yet to come, and Malkuth with the Jewish people.

In a somewhat Freudian twist, Crowley said that the Daughter, after wedding with the Son, becomes the Supernal Mother and the Son replaces the Supernal Father.

DIVISIONS OF THE CABALA

According to S. L. MacGregor Mathers, one of the founders of the Golden Dawn, the cabala can be divided into four classifications: practical, dogmatic, unwritten, and literal. These categories don't seem to be recognized in quite this way by mainstream scholars such as Scholem, but they have been important in the Western Hermetic Tradition since the late 19th century, and, except possibly for the so-called "unwritten" cabala (as defined), they do describe the actual situation.

The practical cabala is concerned with magic, particularly talismans, and is considered the lowest form of this divine science. Indeed, many exponents of the more contemplative forms of cabala quite look down their noses at practical cabalists, as if they represented some sort of perversion of the stainless truth.

Nevertheless, the golem of Prague is perhaps the most famous example of practical cabala. To protect the Jews in the ghetto during a period of persecution, Rabbi Loew created an artificial man made of clay or mud. To animate the creature, he wrote the word "Truth" on the golem's forehead; in Hebrew, *Emeth*, אמת (presumably without Masoretic points). After the golem had gotten out of control, Rabbi Loew destroyed the creature by erasing the letter aleph (א) from its forehead, leaving the word *Meth*, מת, "dead."

The story of the golem is (probably) only a legend, but practical cabala in the form of amulets and talismans has been practiced as long as anyone can determine and is still being practiced today.

Dogmatic cabala might better be called "theoretical" cabala or even "academic" cabala. It consists of the study of the many texts on the subject, such as the *Zohar*.

The unwritten cabala is said to be concerned with the many sets of correspondences that go with the Tree of Life and its 32 paths. Perhaps this is so, but the focus on these correspondences is largely a product of 19th-century eclectic occultism, otherwise typified by H. P. Blavatsky and Albert Pike. Certainly it can no longer be said to be "unwritten," even if it ever was. The main example of the "unwritten" cabala in written form is Crowley's book *Liber 777*, which consists of many columns of correspondences ranging from Hebrew angels to the hexagrams of the *I Ching*. As Mathers observed, there is also a truly unwritten cabala based on a strictly oral tradition. It still remains unwritten partly because of secrecy, but primarily because it is a matter of experience and is not capable of being communicated in writing.

Mathers neglected to mention the widespread use of the cabala for meditation and creative imagination. This is particularly odd when you consider that the cabala had its beginnings, or some of its beginnings, in the *merkabah* mysticism of the first century CE. *Merkabah* means "chariot," such as the flaming chariot of Elijah, which the mystic uses to ascend to the throne of God.

Oddly enough, the Biblical passage describing Elijah's ascent into heaven does not use the word *merkabah*, but rather an abbreviated form of it, *rekeb*, which is a more general term that can also mean "wagon." A *merkabah* is specifically a riding chariot or war chariot, which I suppose is more appropriate for "storming the gates of heaven," as any form of active mysticism is sometimes called.

Merkabah mysticism seems to have consisted of astral journeys through the seven heavens to the throne of God. People still do something similar with a technique called "pathworking."

In pathworking, which is preferably a guided experience for the novice, the student takes an imaginative journey along the paths of the Tree of Life, from Sephirah to Sephirah. The agreed-upon correspondences of the Sephiroth and paths are important for these journeys, as they help to locate you in the right place.

Perhaps somewhat more traditional is the cabalistic method of meditation, which consists primarily of meditation by using the holy names of God as mantras—words or phrases repeated over and over, either silently or whispered, in order to focus the attention and eliminate distractions.

In its earliest beginnings, cabala (which was not yet what we now know as cabala) seems to have included only two divisions: *ma'aseh merkabah* (the way of the chariot, with scriptural study centering on the first chapter of Ezekiel) and *ma'aseh bereshith* (which specialized in the study of the first chapter of Genesis). Both of these schools undoubtedly practiced meditation, if not astral tripping. Except for the magic of the practical cabala, these are the only divisions of the tradition recognized by Scholem.

The literal cabala is based on the idea that scripture can be interpreted by analyzing the words and letters themselves, quite apart from the obvious meaning of the text. The most common form of literal cabala is *gematria*, a word that comes from the Greek *geometria*. This practice no doubt arose from the fact that each Hebrew letter is also a number (see table on page 5). The Romans, who also lacked separate characters for numbers, used I for one, V for five, X for ten and so on, but the Hebrews used every letter in their alphabet, adapting it to the decimal system in a much more practical fashion than the clumsy Roman system.

As a result of this fact, any Hebrew word is also a number. The most straightforward way to write the number 418, for example, would be חית, *cheth*, which is also a word meaning a fence or enclosure and which is, in fact, the name of the eighth letter of the alphabet. With different vowels, by the way, it is *chayyoth*, a word translated in the first chapter of Genesis as "beast." (The number 418 was highly significant in the mystical writings of Aleister Crowley, who identified himself with the beast 666 of the Revelation. However, even he seems to have missed this meaning of חית.)

But numbers do not have to be written in the simplest way possible; any combination of letters that adds up to a number also represents that number. It is considered very significant that אהבה, *ahbah*, "love," and אחד, *echad*, "unity," are both 13, although the simplest way to write 13 is גי. The love = unity = 13 equivalence is considered especially significant because 13 + 13 = 26 = יהוה, Tetragrammaton, the most holy name of God.

Gematria has also been used to explain puzzling passages in scripture. In fact, that was originally the primary purpose of all phases of the literal cabala. In common with similar traditions in other religions, the written word of the holy books is thought to be too sacred to be limited to its obvious, literal meaning. If poetry composed by human beings can have two or more levels of meaning, if only by means of crude double-entendre or puns, then surely any divine revelation must have many depths of significance beyond the prosaic facts that it seems to relate. That meaning may be present and primary, or it may be thought to apply only as an exoteric doctrine for "the great unwashed," but in either case, for the wise, deeper levels of meaning exist.

In fact, four levels of meaning have been postulated for the Torah: the literal, the allegorical, the hermeneutical, and the mystical. Beyond that, it is said to contain infinite depths of meaning—or, anticipating deconstructionist literary criticism, a different meaning for each person who reads it. In this case, however, that *is* the authorial intent.

The obvious way to uncover some of these deeper meanings is meditation, particularly meditation that uses one of the holy names of God as a mantra. Another method, however, both cruder and more sophisticated than meditation, is the analysis of scripture by the literal cabala. It is cruder because it is strictly mechanical and "left-brained" in its approach; it is more sophisticated because it is much more involved and complex than simply sitting and being.

A classic example of gematria as a means of scriptural explanation is that relative to Genesis 18:2, where Abraham is sitting in front of his tent. "And he lifted up his eyes and looked, and lo, three men stood by him: and when he saw them, he ran to meet them from the tent door, and bowed himself toward the ground." Verse 3 goes on to say, "And said, My Lord, if now I have found favor in thy sight, pass not away, I pray thee, from thy servant:" What explains this odd behavior, and why do the three men proceed to deliver messages from God? Who were they? This is explained by gematria. The part that says "and lo, three" in Hebrew is והנה שלשה, *ve-hineh shelshah*. These letters add up to 701. But 701 is also the sum of אלו מיכאל גבריאל ורפאל, "These are Michael, Gabriel, and Raphael."

As another, simpler example, the Hebrew word for "ladder" *(sellam)* and "Sinai" are both equal to 130. This shows that the ladder to heaven—i.e., Jacob's ladder—is provided by the Law given on Sinai.

It should be emphasized that, contrary to a common misconception often expressed in print, two words with the same numerical value are *not* interchangeable or identical. They are not even necessarily synonyms. There is merely an important relationship of some kind between them, and they help to explain each other.

This is not all nonsense. There is very definite evidence that large parts of the Hebrew scriptures were written with a full knowledge of gematria. The two pillars on the porch of the temple of Solomon, Jachin and Boaz (I Kings 7:21) are both equal to 79. Various names of God equal 15 (Yah), 26 (YHVH), 31 (El), and 86 (Elohim). Counting from the beginning, the 15th letter of Genesis is *aleph* (א), which has a value of One, signifying God. The 26th letter, the 31st letter, and the 86th letter are also *aleph*. There are countless examples like this.

Other divisions of the literal cabala include *temurah* and *notariqon*. Temurah is essentially the science of cipher codes. The most famous of these codes is called *Aiq Bekar*, after the first six letters. According to Aiq Bekar, an *aleph*, which has a value of 1, can be written as either *yod* (10) or *qoph* (100), and vice versa. A *beth* (2) can be written as either *kaph* (20) or *resh* (200), and so on through *teth* (9), *tzaddi* (90), and final *tzaddi* (900). The table of Aiq Bekar is shown below:

ג ל ש	ב כ ר	א י ק
ו ס ם	ה נ ך	ד מ ת
ט צ ץ	ח פ ף	ז ע ן

So by this method a word such as תורה, *torah*, law, can be written in an enciphered form as מסבך, *misbakh*, a maze. If you consider all the depths of the Torah, which is another name for the Pentateuch or Five Books of Moses (Genesis, Exodus, Leviticus, Numbers, and Deuteronomy), you will have to thread a complicated maze, but there is a priceless treasure at the center.

Notariqon is the cabalistic science of anagrams. By this method, the letters of one word are taken to stand for a phrase, or the initial of the words in a phrase are taken together to form one word. An example of notariqon is the word for grace, *chen*, חן, formed from the initials of *chokmah nisetarah*, secret wisdom. A Christian example of notariqon, using the Greek language, is the word *ichthys*, fish, which is taken to be an anagram for *Iesous Christos theos huios soter* (Jesus Christ, son of God, savior). A stylized fish was an early Christian symbol.

THE PATHS

To return to the Tree, the Sephiroth are connected by the 22 paths or channels (connecting lines), which correspond to the 22 letters of the Hebrew alphabet. In the seventeenth century, a document appeared, attached to the *Sepher Yetzirah* as if an original part of it, called "The Thirty-Two Paths of Wisdom." This text speaks of each path as being an "intelligence" (*sekhel*) and then describes it in rather cryptic terms;

for example, "The Twenty-sixth Path [i.e., Tiphareth to Hod] is called the Renovating Intelligence, because the Holy God renews by it all the changing things which are renewed by the creation of the world" (Westcott's translation of 1911). Many occultists claim to find this document extremely helpful.

The letters were attributed to the paths of the Tree by the Golden Dawn adepts as shown in the diagram on page 11. This is the system that is in almost universal use today for path-working, the Hermetic cabala, and ceremonial magic. It was the system used by MacGregor Mathers, Aleister Crowley, and Dion Fortune. It is used today by BOTA and other organizations that had their origins associated with the Golden Dawn.

Crowley's "magical son," Charles Stansfield Jones ("Frater Achad") was inspired to revamp the system from bottom to top, with *aleph* assigned to the 32nd path and *tau* to the 11th, although he retained the correspondences of the path numbers with the letters by renumbering the paths from bottom to top. For example, Achad's "11th Path" *(aleph)* runs from Malkuth to Yesod. Crowley thought this method was nonsense involving "supreme atrocities," but it has its merits, and some groups now working use this method.

In 1936, C. C. Zain (i.e., Elbert Benjamine), founder of the Brotherhood of Light, brought out an entirely different system that more or less ignored the astrological and planetary attributions according to mother, double, and single letters. Zain's system was keyed to the Tarot rather than to the Tree, however.

Despite all this, the assignment of the letters to the paths made by the great cabalist Isaac Luria in the sixteenth century probably makes more sense than either of these and is much more elegant and appealing. He put the three mother letters on the three horizontal paths of the Tree, the seven double letters on the seven vertical paths, and the 12 single letters on the 12 diagonal paths. Isaac's version of the Tree is also slightly different. He had only one path leading to Malkuth (the one from Yesod), but he had paths connecting Chokmah with Geburah and Binah with Chesed. This also makes more sense, as it provides a path for the Lightning Flash and indicates that following the path of the Middle Pillar is the only way you can even begin to approach God. Even in the Golden Dawn, the 30th and 31st paths were closed to the Neophyte.

Isaac Luria's Tree is shown on page 44, and the table on pages 42–43 shows the assignment of the elements, planets, and signs to the letters

ATTRIBUTIONS OF THE LETTERS

Letter	Golden Dawn Attribution	Path**	Sepher Yetzirah* Attribution	Path
Aleph	Air	11	Air	19
Beth	Mercury	12	Saturn	16
Gimel	Moon	13	Jupiter	18
Daleth	Venus	14	Mars	13
Heh	Aries	15	Aries	11
Vau	Taurus	16	Taurus	12
Zayin	Gemini	17	Gemini	(2–5)**
Cheth	Cancer	18	Cancer	20
Teth	Leo	19	Leo	15
Yod	Virgo	20	Virgo	24
Kaph	Jupiter	21	Sun	21
Lamed	Libra	22	Libra	30
Mem	Water	23	Water	27
Nun	Scorpio	24	Scorpio	28
Samekh	Sagittarius	25	Sagittarius	26
Ayin	Capricorn	26	Capricorn	17
Peh	Mars	27	Venus	23
Tzaddi	Aquarius	28	Aquarius	22
Qoph	Pisces	29	Pisces	(3–4)**
Resh	Sun	30	Mercury	25
Shin	Fire	31	Fire	14
Tau	Saturn	32	Moon	32

*This information was added at a much later date and cannot be said to be a part of the original *Sepher Yetzirah*. Furthermore, there are various extant versions of the planetary attributions. The primary variation is Beth-Moon, Gimel-Mars, Daleth-Sun, Kaph-Venus, Peh-Mercury, Resh-Saturn, and Tau-Jupiter.

**There seems to be no evidence that Isaac Luria used the same path numbers that the Golden Dawn used, and some evidence that he used entirely different numbers based on the attributions of the 32 paths to the 32 mentions of Elohim in Genesis 1. Nevertheless, for the sake of establishing some sort of standard reference system within this booklet, the more familiar path numbering of the Golden Dawn (see p. 11) is used here in all instances.

Be that as it may, there are two paths on the Luria Tree that do not exist on the Golden Dawn Tree. These are indicated in the table by "2–5" (Chokmah to Geburah) and "3–4" (Binah to Chesed).

ATTRIBUTIONS OF THE LETTERS (cont'd.)

Letter	Frater Achad Attribution	Path*	C.C. Zain Attribution	Tarot**
Aleph	Air	32 (11)	Mercury	Magician
Beth	Mercury	31 (12)	Virgo	Priestess
Gimel	Moon	30 (13)	Libra	Empress
Daleth	Venus	29 (14)	Scorpio	Emperor
Heh	Aries	22 (21)	Jupiter	Hierophant
Vau	Taurus	27 (16)	Venus	Lovers
Zayin	Gemini	26 (17)	Sagittarius	Chariot
Cheth	Cancer	28 (15)	Capricorn	Justice
Teth	Leo	24 (19)	Aquarius	Hermit
Yod	Virgo	23 (20)	Uranus	Fortune
Kaph	Jupiter	11 (32)	Neptune	Strength
Lamed	Libra	21 (22)	Pisces	Hanged Man
Mem	Water	25 (18)	Aries	Death
Nun	Scorpio	19 (24)	Taurus	Temperance
Samekh	Sagittarius	16 (27)	Saturn	Devil
Ayin	Capricorn	17 (26)	Mars	Tower
Peh	Mars	18 (25)	Gemini	Star
Tzaddi	Aquarius	14 (29)	Cancer	Moon
Qoph	Pisces	20 (23)	Leo	Sun
Resh	Sun	15 (28)	Moon	Judgment
Shin	Fire	13 (30)	Sun	World
Tau	Saturn	12 (31)	Earth/ Pluto	Fool

*The numbers in parentheses represent Achad's renumbering of the paths, which he outlined in *Q.B.L. or The Bride's Reception*. In *The Egyptian Revival*, however, he abandoned path numbers altogether.

**Zain's titles for the Tarot trumps were, of course, entirely different (e.g., The Chariot = The Conqueror), but I have used more-or-less standard titles to avoid confusion.

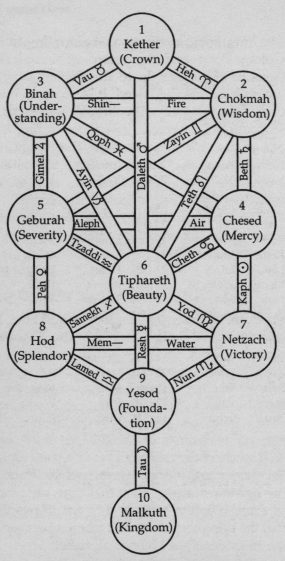

The Tree of Life according to Isaac Luria

(the "Yetziratic attributions") according to the Golden Dawn and also according to most versions of the addenda to the *Sepher Yetzirah*, which Isaac also followed. It is not true, however, that the Tree with three paths going to Malkuth is a Christian invention. In fact, it is one of the oldest forms of the Tree. Logically, Christians should prefer the Tree that shows only "one way" from Malkuth, that which leads through Yesod to Jesus in Tiphareth.

The table on page 43 shows the Yetziratic attributions according to Frater Achad and according to C. C. Zain.

THE CABALA AND THE TAROT

There are 22 letters in the Hebrew alphabet. By coincidence or design, there are also 22 trump cards in a Tarot deck. It is not as improbable as it might at first seem to think that the "coincidence" was deliberate. It is not necessary that the Tarot should have been designed by a council of wise men in Morocco for this to be so. The Platonic revivalists of Renaissance Italy were well aware of the cabala and the Hebrew alphabet, thanks to the work of men such as Ficino. If the Tarot were designed at that time and place, as some scholars believe, it is not impossible that the designers created 22 trumps because of the 22 letters of the Hebrew alphabet.

Unfortunately, there has been very little agreement for the last 150 years or so about which trump goes with which letter, even less so than with the planets. The table on the following page shows various versions of the correspondences between Tarot trumps and the Hebrew letters. Achad followed Crowley's system, which at that time was the same as the system of the Golden Dawn; he just renumbered the paths from bottom to top. Zain used the letter-card correspondences of Eliphas Levi except for transposing the last two (The World and The Fool); it was just his astrological attributions that were different.

The Golden Dawn adepts worked out a quite elaborate system of correspondences based on the Tarot attributions that they used within the Order. These were supposedly based on information in the so-called cipher manuscripts, papers variously said to have been discovered in a Masonic library, found in a bookstall, unearthed from the manuscript collection of Kenneth Mackenzie, or forged by Wynn Westcott. As may be seen from the table, these attributions are totally at odds with those of Levi, which had been widely accepted in occult circles until that time.

In any case, the Golden Dawn attributions—as elaborated and expanded by Aleister Crowley and/or by BOTA founder Paul Foster

TAROT ATTRIBUTIONS

Letter	Levi	Golden Dawn	Crowley
Aleph	Magician	Fool	Fool
Beth	Priestess	Magician	Magician
Gimel	Empress	Priestess	Priestess
Daleth	Emperor	Empress	Empress
Heh	Hierophant	Emperor	Star
Vau	Lovers	Hierophant	Hierophant
Zayin	Chariot	Lovers	Lovers
Cheth	Justice	Chariot	Chariot
Teth	Hermit	Strength	Strength
Yod	Wheel	Hermit	Hermit
Kaph	Strength	Wheel	Wheel
Lamed	Hanged Man	Justice	Justice
Mem	Death	Hanged Man	Hanged Man
Nun	Temperance	Death	Death
Samekh	Devil	Temperance	Temperance
Ayin	Tower	Devil	Devil
Peh	Star	Tower	Tower
Tzaddi	Moon	Star	Emperor
Qoph	Sun	Moon	Moon
Resh	Judgment	Sun	Sun
Shin	Fool	Judgment	Judgment
Tau	World	World	World

As noted before, Zain's attributions agree with Levi's except for transposing The Fool (tau) and The World (shin).

Crowley, of course, renamed some of the trumps to fit his own magical system; e.g., Strength was renamed Lust. However, this booklet is not the place to discuss Tarot terminology.

Case—are now used almost universally. From an objective point of view, these attributions are as "correct" as any other. The criterion is not accuracy according to some absolute truth—which, because all such systems of attribution are somewhat arbitrary, does not exist in this case—but rather usefulness to the individual who is working with it. Many people feel more comfortable working with the Tarot without any reference whatever to the cabala or the Tree, and, if the truth were known, they might be the ones who are really being the most faithful to the authentic tradition.

THE LURIANIC CABALA

In the sixteenth century, Isaac Luria introduced several innovative ideas into the cabala. These have been largely ignored in the Western Hermetic Tradition, probably because Luria lived long after the cabala had been popularized in Christian circles by Reuchlin, Agrippa, and so on. The Elizabethan magus John Dee, for example, was apparently unaware of Luria's ideas, and they are not to be found in the published literature of the Golden Dawn. The lack of Lurianic content in the tradition of the West may also be due to the depth and complexity of his ideas, some of which are very difficult to understand without actual mystical experience.

The most revolutionary idea that Luria produced was that of *tzimtzum*—contraction. Instead of the universe being produced by emanation from God, rather like the light from a light bulb, Luria thought that God had to contract His essence to make room for something less than Himself. What to us is the dazzling light of Kether is but darkness to God.

After *tzimtzum*, the light of God illuminated the vacated space and produced Adam Qadmon, who is above the Four Worlds, and the Sephiroth took shape within him. Lights shining forth from the head of Adam Qadmon filled the vessels of the Sephiroth, but, due to a rather complex imbalance, this light was just too much for some of the lower Sephiroth (below the Supernals), and the vessels were shattered. This is how the evil demons *(qlippoth)* and matter itself originated.

Luria's cabala is primarily concerned with the problem of repairing the damage in a process of reintegration called *tikkun*. Part of this restoration, which takes place by means of the light of Adam Qadmon, is accomplished by means of his *partzuphim*, or "faces," which are apparently something like the unbroken essences or forms of the Sephiroth. Meanwhile, the task of humanity is to restore the World of Assiah to spirituality.

This has necessarily been a very brief and superficial description of the Lurianic cabala. A more detailed discussion occurs in *Kabbalah* by Gershom Scholem (1974), currently in print by Dorset Press.

PRACTICAL APPLICATIONS

The only practical use of the cabala of which traditional cabalists approve is to advance oneself spiritually, through study and through meditation on the names of God. Even pathworking, as it is usually practiced by New Age aficionados, would be considered superficial and demeaning. Serious students and practitioners, whether they be traditional cabalists or Native American shamans, tend to cast a jaundiced eye on the tendency of certain shallow enthusiasts to co-opt sacred traditions and turn them into a pastime like bingo or a hobby like needlepoint. Ascending the Path of the Serpent, if it is to be anything but an idle daydream, is a serious business requiring many years of intelligently and persistently applied study and practice.

To deal with the sacred letters in a frivolous fashion is to invite disaster—or so go the warnings issued by the traditionalists. At the same time, the average person who does not wish to devote a lifetime exclusively to cabala can derive some use from it simply by understanding something about it.

There is some evidence that the subconscious mind understands the basis of cabala even if you have never studied it or even read about it. That is because cabala deals with archetypal energies, and cabalistic imagery is one way of approaching an understanding of such energies. For example, dreams often make use of cabalistic symbolism, even to the point of presenting puns and analogies to be understood only by gematria.

A book of gematria values, such as *Godwin's Cabalistic Encyclopedia* (Llewellyn, 1994) or *The Spice of Torah—Gematria* by Gutman G. Locks (Judaica Press, 1985), can be used as a reference for divination, much as the Bible has been used for divination by opening it at random and pointing at a verse. Naturally, there are people who object to the use of such holy objects for such mundane purposes, but the opposing theory states that religion and mysticism are not truly valid or relevant if they fail to address the problems of everyday living. In any case, you can carry out a divination with a book of gematria by generating a random three-digit number by means of dice or a computer and then looking up the number in the book to get a key word or words that relates to the question at hand.

You can also derive a value for a person's name by substituting Hebrew letters for the letters of the English alphabet, but personally I have not found this technique to be particularly useful or meaningful.

The premier practical application of the knowledge (if not the wisdom) of the cabala, however, has always been ceremonial magic, particularly the making and charging of amulets and talismans. A good description of how to approach this particular magical art is given in *Modern Magick* by Donald Michael Kraig (Llewellyn, 1988).

Another practical application of cabala within the field of magic is the use of gematria to test the validity of experiences and the authenticity of spirits. This technique is described at greater length in *Godwin's Cabalistic Encyclopedia*.

Whether you see cabala as a magical tool or as a strictly mystical philosophy, a thorough study of the subject will repay the time spent and enrich your life immeasurably.

STAY IN TOUCH

On the following pages you will find some of the books now available on related subjects. Your book dealer stocks most of these and will stock new titles in the Llewellyn series as they become available. We urge your patronage.

To obtain our full catalog write for our bimonthly news magazine/catalog, *Llewellyn's New Worlds of Mind and Spirit*. A sample copy is free, and it will continue coming to you at no cost as long as you are an active mail customer. Or you may subscribe for just $10.00 in the U.S.A. and Canada ($20.00 overseas, first class mail). Many bookstores also have *New Worlds* available to their customers. Ask for it.

Llewellyn's New Worlds of Mind and Spirit
P.O. Box 64383-K325, St. Paul, MN 55164-0383, U.S.A.

TO ORDER BOOKS AND TAPES

If your book dealer does not have the books described, you may order them directly from the publisher by sending full price in U.S. funds, plus $3.00 for postage and handling for orders under $10.00; $4.00 for orders over $10.00. There are no postage and handling charges for orders over $50.00. Postage and handling rates are subject to change. We ship UPS whenever possible. Delivery guaranteed. Provide your street address as UPS does not deliver to P.O. Boxes. UPS to Canada requires a $50.00 minimum order. Allow 4-6 weeks for delivery. Orders outside the U.S.A. and Canada: Airmail—add retail price of book; add $5.00 for each non-book item (tapes, etc.); add $1.00 per item for surface mail. Mail orders to:

LLEWELLYN PUBLICATIONS
P.O. Box 64383-K325, St. Paul, MN 55164-0383, U.S.A.

Prices subject to change without notice.

GODWIN'S CABALISTIC ENCYCLOPEDIA
Complete Guidance to Both Practical and Esoteric Applications
by David Godwin

One of the most valuable books on the Cabala is back, with a new and more usable format. This book is a complete guide to cabalistic magick and gematria in which every demon, angel, power, and name of God ... every Sephiroth, Path, and Plane of the Tree of Life ... and each attribute and association is fully described and cross-indexed by the Hebrew, English, and numerical forms.

All entries, which had been scattered throughout the appendices, are now incorporated into one comprehensive dictionary. There are hundreds of new entries and illustrations, making this book even more valuable for Cabalistic pathworking and meditation. It now has many new Hebrew words and names, as well as the terms of Freemasonry, the entities of the Cthulhu mythos, and the Aurum Solis spellings for the names of the demons of the Goetia. It contains authentic Hebrew spellings, and a new introduction that explains the uses of the book for meditation on God names.

The Cabalistic schema is native to the human psyche, and *Godwin's Cabalistic Encyclopedia* will be a valuable reference tool for all Cabalists, magicians, scholars, and scientists of all disciplines.

1–56718–324–7, 832 pgs., 6 x 9, softcover $24.95

MAGICAL GATEWAYS
by Alan Richardson
Originally published as *An Introduction to the Mystical Qabalah* (1974, 1981), *Magical Gateways* is the revised and substantially expanded re-release of of this excellent introduction to the essentials of magic.

It shows magic to be a spiritual system which everyone can use to enhance their lives. Whatever your spiritual path, these tried-and-tested methods will expand your consciousness and broaden your grasp of the Western Esoteric Tradition as it exists today.

Explore the theories and principles behind ritual practice (i.e., the Middle Pillar and the Lesser Banishing Ritual) that other books only touch upon. Explore the Qabalah—the Tree of Life—as it applies to daily living, perform astral magic, use the Tarot for self-exploration, relate mythology to your own life to gain greater self-knowledge, revisit past lives, build patterns in your aura, banish unpleasant atmospheres, and create gates into other dimensions.

This is the world of *real* magic, in which an understanding of the Qabalah forms the first step in a radical transformation of personal consciousness.

0-87542-681-6, 208 pgs., mass market, illus.   **$4.95**

SIMPLIFIED MAGIC
A Beginner's Guide to the New Age Qabala
by Ted Andrews

In every person, the qualities essential for accelerating his or her growth and spiritual evolution are innate, but even those who recognize such potentials need an effective means of releasing them. The ancient and mystical Qabala is that means.

A person does not need to become a dedicated Qabalist in order to acquire benefits from the Qabala. *Simplified Magic* offers a simple understanding of what the Qabala is and how it operates. It provides practical methods and techniques so that the energies and forces within the system and within ourselves can be experienced in a manner that enhances growth and releases our greater potential. A reader knowing absolutely nothing about the Qabala could apply the methods in this book with noticeable success!

The Qabala is more than just some theory for ceremonial magicians. It is a system for personal attainment and magic that anyone can learn and put to use in his or her life. The secret is that the main glyph of the Qabala, the Tree of Life, is within you. The Tree of Life is a map to the levels of consciousness, power and magic that are within. By learning the Qabala, you will be able to tap into these levels and bring peace, healing, power, love, light, and magic into your life.

0-87542-015-X, 208 pgs., mass market, illus. $3.95

THE MIDDLE PILLAR
by Israel Regardie

Between the two outer pillars of the Qabalistic Tree of Life, the extremes of Mercy and Severity, stands *The Middle Pillar*, signifying one who has achieved equilibrium in his or her own self.

Integration of the human personality is vital to the continuance of creative life. Without it, man lives as an outsider to his own true self. By combining Magic and Psychology in the Middle Pillar Ritual/Exercise (a magical meditation technique), we bring into balance the opposing elements of the psyche while yet holding within their essence and allowing full expression of man's being.

In this book, and with this practice, you will learn to: understand the psyche through its correspondences of the Tree of Life; expand self-awareness, thereby intensifying the inner growth process; activate creative and intuitive potentials; understand the individual thought patterns which control every facet of personal behavior; and regain the sense of balance and peace of mind—the equilibrium that everyone needs for phsyical and psychic health.

0-87542-658-1, 176 pgs., 5¼ x 8 softcover $8.95

LIGHT IN EXTENSION
Greek Magic from Homer to Modern Times
by David Godwin

Greek magic is the foundation of almost every form of ceremonial magic being practiced today. Elements of Greek philosophy summarize the bulk of modern esoteric thought and occult teachings. Even the cabala contains many features that appear to be Greek in origin. The systems formulated by the direct progenitors of Western culture speak to the modern soul of the Western world.

This book explains in plain, informal language the grand sweep of Greek magic and Greek philosophical and religious concepts from the archaic period of Homer's *Iliad* right down to the present. It begins with the magic and mythology of the days of classical Athens and its antecedent cultures, gives detailed considerations of Gnosticism, early Christianity and Neoplatonism—all phenomena with a Greek foundation—explains the manifestations of Greek thought in the Renaissance, and explores modern times with the Greek elements of the magic of the Golden Dawn, Aleister Crowley, and others.

For the practicing magician, rituals are given that incorporate elements from each historical period that is discussed. These ceremonies may be easily adapted for Pagan or Wiccan practice or otherwise altered to suit the individual operator.

From the plains of Troy to the streets of Los Angeles, Greek magic is alive and well. No one who has any interest in magic, occultism, or hermetic thought and who is also a citizen of Western civilization can afford to ignore this heritage.

0–87542–285–3, 272 pgs., 6 x 9, illus., softcover   **$12.95**